# *Acts of Creation*

*the poetry of*
CRAIG WILLIAM ANDREWS

*Acts of
Creation*

An effulgent publication of
**AUTUMN SUN PUBLISHING**
Sequim, Washington

Acts of Creation
by Craig William Andrews

Copyright © 2014 by Craig William Andrews
All rights reserved.
Printed in the United States of America

*Published by*
Craig Andrews / Autumn Sun Publishing
tarasparkman@yahoo.com

Typestyle: Sabon
Book Design by Ruth Marcus, Rmarcus@olypen.com
Illustration on Half Title Page by Craig William Andrews

No part of this book may be used or reproduced
in any manner whatsoever without the written
permission of the author.

ISBN 978-0692263-68-6

*Dedication*

For Tara.
Fierce editor,
Beauty and Love,
all in one package.

## Table of Contents

xi Preface
xiii Theme

POETRY
1 The Birth of the Thunderbird
3 Four Element Theory
7 Epiphany
8 Confluence
9 Mist Through a Grove
10 An Old Man With a Violin In a Hall Filled with Aficionados of the Art
11 Ode to Tara, My Light – My Wife
12 I Have Found My Way Home Again
13 Confabulation With My Self
15 No Place Other Than Me
16 In the Power of the Word
17 Kristina's Health
20 O
22 Full Moon at a Deserted Estate in Santa Barbara
21 For My Father
24 Kali in Morning Light

25 In Poppy Dreams
26 Integration
27 In the Beginning
29 Forgetting to Re-Member
30 Manifesto
31 Twelve Steps to Life
32 Transference
34 4 AM
34 September
35 Three Poems for the Almost Full Moon of a January Night
38 The Flavor of Me
39 Mother Tara Who Has a Heart as Big as the Sky
40 I Will
41 The Guiding Force
42 The Nature of What is Lost
44 Natural Selection
45 Pennyweight in Browser
46 Left Turn to the Center
47 Seeking a Planetary Presence
48 In the Realm of Hungry Ghosts
49 Preface to Monsoon
50 Monsoon

## *Preface*

I Am rooted in this Earth. Besot with Her. A Born
Again Earthling. Many of my Poems reflect this
reverence, But I Am also a-mused with the
contradictions which I find in the very foundations
of Life; what some might call the basic absurdities
of Life. My mind soars with these and I
cannot help but ask questions which cannot be
answered, or assert impossible statements as though
they were facts, as if my stating of them could
make them so.
Words have power. Poetry is powerful –
transformative. At its best it walks the lines of
Reality reshaping it at will.
It is difficult to find relevance in what cannot
be explained, but poetry, like all fine arts, has a
way of molding the unexplainable, giving it a flavor
a substance, which may be digested into the psyche.
And so I tender these poems to you. A gift from my
own deeper place to your own deeper place, and it is
my wish that they settle well in you.

Craig Andrews

## *Theme*

In the first golden dawn,
The Over Soul that was the Nation of Woman
    and Man
Stopped before the Throne of Heaven
And God spoke from out of the depths of the
    Throne,
"For what reason have I become you forever
    becoming me?
For what reason have I given you a mind set free
    to wander?
And for what reason are you a child born of
    My Infinity?"
And then that Wondrous Flame of Life,
Which is the Over Soul of Woman and Man,
Lifted its eyes into the Glory of the Throne
And recited a poem of its own making,
And God sighed,
And Beauty flickered within his Breath
And a tear of Amber dropped into the void
Which became a Universe filled with Worlds
For Worlds were born from that poem;
And from that dawning day into this Endless Now
That poem has never ceased in its telling
But constantly births anew through the timeless
    lineage of the Bard,
Through the gift of the Poet
Through the gift of the Muse.

## *The Birth of the Firebird*

When there is nothing,
Really nothing,
Then there is no place for any thing to come from,
So when a spot of intelligence appears,
It comes from no place at all,
But once it is here
"Nothing," can no longer exist
And that little spot of intelligence
Is something which is brilliantly alive
In an empty Universe that is completely Other,
But somehow supports a feeling of buoyancy
Which holds up wings
And a Heart which yearns
So that it sings,
And when it sings it finds itself
Flying into a golden light
In which the light is like clay
And it forms with the notes of the song
Into the features of a world,
Mountains, and ponds,
And seas which give into grasslands
That pass beneath its feathered breast
In the dawning light of a new world,
And all the myriad Beings awake and blink
    their eyes,

Or swim through the medium of blood and bone
Or seal their time and self
Into the crystals of the earth,
And wind their way through their own
Tales of Creation
While the shadow of the Thunderbird
Passes over the land
Her call fills the Heavens
lightning flashes in the blink of Her eyes
And the earth shakes within the thunder of
    Her wings,
While all Things are made anew.

## *Four Element Theory*

### *Canto I – Fire*

On a Winter Solstice morning, the Sun returned
A radiant fire
Blessing to all who could see,
Life affirming warmth to all who could feel its light
    upon their skin,
And the world became alive in the brilliance of the Sun,
In Light the Sacred Dance began,
And living in this Light
There was some deep smile
Some All-Intensive Intelligence in Whom this
    whole wide Universe has expressed itself in the
    continuance of a Soul
So that within this expression of Fire
The Angels came to grow
And they cast lots upon Eternities ground to see whom
    will descend to whom
To spread the power of wonder upon the Fields of Life
And all this within a Winter Solstice Sunrise
In flames of rose and gold.

## Canto II – Air

There are things which live in the air,
They move in the air and it is solid beneath them
Like water or earth,
And there are some things which live in the air but
    cannot be seen
Perhaps as Angels
Perhaps as Spirits of another kind,
And there are spaces where air is an emptiness
 between two things
A river of No-thing which allows for Some-thing
    to exist,
To be seen,
And it is through the Air that the Song of Heaven
    lays upon the Earth
Lapis Blue,
And the scents and feelings which tell the Earth of
    our love for Her,
And we breathe-in the Air to fan the fire at the
    center of the world
Which is the center of our Heart
The Navel to which we traveled so long ago,
For in the Air we can Dance
But without the Air we cannot move.

## Canto III – Earth

The Earth has enough moods to fill the Universe
 with Stars
She is emotional,
And through Her Humanness She is crafting
 a Heart;

There is a cleanliness
An objectivity which is perceived in the minds
 of men
 as they study The Laws of Heaven,
They would conceive of an orderly world,
But this will never happen
Because the Earth – Our Mother,
Is a woman in – love.

## Canto IV – Water

It is said that our tears mimic the sea from which
Life was born,
But perhaps the sea mimics the tears of Life
    birthing a world?
And Water is the Great Mystery
Because, like energy,
Water can not be made or destroyed
So there is that part of everything
Which is a very large part of Everything
Which is water,
But perhaps, all things are merely Here
So that Water may have a home.
For The Light was Pure Intelligence,
It had no words, and it had no life
It could be anything at all

But it had to wait to be noticed,
It had to wait for Me to evolve.

## *Epiphany*

I sing my body,
This life
This dance which grapples with Being,
A miracle,
If only I could understand the power of that word,
And words build power out of understanding,
Understanding out of what?
Out of a blackness which covers the place in which
    they live
My brain a blackness which covers the place in
    which they hide,
Hide until they ride forth,
Meanings riding the currents of a million billion cells
Until they burst forth into my head,
Complete sentences,
complete thoughts,
Whole philosophies of Life,
But each cell is a life of its own,
A Wholeness, Holiness in itself
Or perhaps a mind which is deathless.

## *Confluence*

Where am I in all of this water,
This ocean of Being?
My brain floats in water,
All of my innards float in water,
My blood and my tears have the make-up of a Sea!
I wear my body like a fish wears its pond
Its' aquarium – Its' bowl,
I have grown tubes which connect me to food –
    to drink,
To eliminate my waste so that my water stays clean,
Every cell of me is permeated with water like a true
    believer is permeated with God,
And what is left of Me?
A hand full of minerals
And a tiny filigree of nerve endings like the Earth
 covered with lace
And my thoughts submerged complexities blowing
 bubbles which turn into poems?
And then the Timeless Teachers of Dharma issue forth
    their proclamations
"You are light! You are vibration!
"You are the Infinite Spirit Taking Form in the body of
    your dreams,"
And where? I need to know
Is there room for that? In all this water.

## *Mist Through a Grove*

Last year it snowed and it did not melt
But snowed again,
And again,
And the snow and ice stayed with us forever
Which it should not have done;
And this year, in this same time, it has rained,
And Rained,
And the rain has a Southern warmth about it
Which it should not have,
And so I need to speak to the Wild Things in this
Earthly Life
All of the Things which have only feared me before,
And I need to remind them that Terra is tuning
    Her face
 in a new direction now,
That She knows what She I doing
She knows what She is about,
And we should not be afraid
For no thing is lost within Her Heart
And every rainbow speaks this promise to us
For we are dwellers in Her womb;
This Earth Becoming,
Always becoming new.

## *An Old Man with a Violin in a Hall Filled with Young Aficionados of the Art*

It was a simple etude,
A small fleck of music,
But it did not seem to have a beginning,
That is,
One could not remember when he began to play
    his first note,
Nor did it seem to have an ending,
That is,
One could not remember an ending,
Only that he wasn't playing any longer
And in-between these to indefinite points
An infinity of Beauty,
A Timeless weaving,
And a sweetness of Character
That eludes capture.

*Ode to Tara*
*My Light – My Wife*

I live in a world where the Heavens are blue,
My Soul Embedded in a Great Blueness,
In blue waters
And the soft blue of dreams of you;

I Am blessed in the gentle blue/white of clouds
And the turquoise of mountain streams,
The opalescence of dragonfly wings
And the blue/green of your Irish eyes,
I will live forever beyond the reds and greens of angers
    and jealousies
And settle within the deep indigo of your sighs.

## I Have Found My Way Home Again

In the greening of the leaves
In the trees which freely breathe into the starry night,
In the fields
Open to where my eyes rest against the line of sky and mountain
Huge and distant and blue,
And the wind which bends the grasslands
And sings all the way into the center of my bones,
I am vested in the sureness of where I belong,
I AM Earthling Born,
I do not want to pass into Heavens of Pure Lands of Omniscient Making,
I need to feel the squish of mud between my toes
I need to fart and laugh while small birds race from bush to bush
And coyotes warble in the evening light,
I want to poke my head into every nook and cranny of this hoary world
And exchange pleasantries with creatures that look like knobby branches,
I do not need technological wonders,
I need the wonder of a God
bent down with dirt between his hands.

## Confabulation with My Self

"Self," I said to me,
How can I be at home in this Immensity?
How can I when I know that each second,
Every second!
Which measures my life
My Earthly existence
Is born from out of the Womb of Eternity
To return to Eternity
Taking with it one more stolen second of my fleshy
    existence
One more bite of my time in this Earth,
My Time!
In where?
In what?
I do not know where I Am
(only names for it)
I do not know what I Am
(again, only names for it)
I only know,
Really know,
That, I Am
Not because I think that I Am
But because I feel my self,

And if I weren't constantly distracted from this only
    one real point of existence which is the feeling of me
If I weren't constantly distracted from this point in
    consciousness
I would be totally lost in the wonder of it all,
I would be standing, slack-jawed, wide-eyed,
    gaping, and drooling
Until they carried me off and put me on a feeding tube,
I mean,
How can this be!

How can any thing come out of no thing?
How can anything be measured against infinity?
Like Forever was the bread and I was the lunch meat?
All of this is beginning to add up to impossibilities
Maya, Wizardry, Spells,
This has nothing to do with science,
This is Enchantment as the Foundation of us all.

## *No Place Other Than Me*

"So you see?"
I say to myself,
It is the power of the word
Which will set me free,
Belief does not come unbidden
But must be coaxed with meaning,
Must hungrily fasten itself
Upon the explanation of some great sagacity,
Sucking the nourishment
That will enable it to grow its wings,
A metamorphosis,
A dragon fly fire force
Born through the waters of my desires,
To fly in the fires of Truth
Swimming to freedom through my ocean of fears,
This must be!
For I will not allow any such thing
As a termination of my Brilliance,
Change is acceptable,
Old age – a transformation into what is new
But not what is other,
Because this whole illuminated Dharma
Has no place to die
No place for it to be anything other that me.

## *In the Power of the Word*

It is in the Realm of the Sacred
That these words are written,
That they flow,
Undiagnosed,
Through the earthy confines of bone, and blood,
    and sinew,
And the manufactured tip of an instrument for
    the transferring of words into chemicals which
    ooze thought and feeling onto the flat surface
    of paper,
Paper!
The wonder of Life has been stretched thin over
    the substantiality of paper,
Which then enters into the eyes of a
Seeker of depth...Of Truth!
And leaps into the Infinity of yet another mind,
Or the same mind looking through yet another set
    of eyes,
Crossing yet another bridge
Into the vastness of its own labyrinth of Wonder
Sailing the waters of its own ecstatic tears
As it screams into the Heavens,
"I want to be Me!...Forever!"
"I want to Believe!"

## Kristina's Health

Health is perhaps a mental condition,
In my minds eye I look to see my self as a healthy
   person
Person?
And Health?
What is that?
It is healthy to be strong and alert
To be agile and emotionally stable
It is also healthy to be financially secure
Isn't it?
And we talk about healthy friendships
Relationships,
We wish to eat healthy food
Live in a healthy environment,
Is it healthy for me to be asking large questions
To be writing this poem?
To talk to my self
To stare at the sky?
We say of each other
He (She) does not live a healthy life,
How would I know to say such a thing
Which life am I talking about?

Which possibility?
How many of us have needed our un-health to
    purchase our view of Paradise?
Our un-health then was our mission to Earth
It was what we came here for,
Is this a curiosity?
Perhaps, like a Peeping Tom,
I have come here out of curiosity.

# O

For just as one small bird is chosen to sing-in the
    new day
I have somehow been chosen to sing-in this
    brightening of Love,
This "Pure Land,"
Lips curved into an O
In wonder as I step lightly as a deer
Quickly – quietly crossing the clearing before the
    hunter can level his gun,
And in the Diamond Chamber there sits a Buddha
Maybe two
One for each side of this great gender divide
Which re-focuses as one thought further out into the
    ocean of life
For such is Beauty – Enchantment – gifted to us
And I AM Becoming Infinity,
Not that I Am
But that I Am Becoming
Where before I was naught
But then there was you
Caught in the loins of my own secret glance.

## *Full Moon at a Deserted Estate in Santa Barbara*

It is there again
Dancing about the fountain on the smooth dewy
    stones
Its eyes sparkling in the moonlight
Its mouth agape in smile
Slack in the pleasure of it all,
I watch from behind the trellis,
There is nothing threatening about it
Yet I am terrified least I be caught
And I don't want it to end
For it dances for me,
Breathing out from that sweet Faerie place
It dances in the enchantment of my heart
Given wings.

## *For My Father*

It is 3 o'clock in the morning
And I Am sitting naked at my desk
Pen in hand
Because the words have come again,
They are here again,
They have rattled about in the back places of
    my mind
Their "someplace" where words live while they
    are waiting to be born
Demanding to be born
Until shivering and blurry-eyed
I have stumbled down the stairs
And into my study shutting the door,
Turn on the light
Stoke-up the heat
And the words flow through me
While others sleep,
While others sleep I transform my self
Becoming what I write,
I Am Anger,
I Am Beauty
I Am the Exploding brilliance of a Star

I Am "That" because my words create me
They are the Dance of Power
And what cannot be described
Does not exist
But what can be described becomes a matrix which
In-forms Me into every cell of my body,
And I re-member my self with every word I speak,
    write, think, or dream,
Well, I Am an Architect
I Am designing the home of my Soul
I Am designing the body of my world
Fleshing them out with the words that I use
Like a child builds a cabin out of Lincoln Logs
Building them up
Making ever more complex structures
And it is like this that Reality embraces my use
    of the language
Pouring itself into molds of meanings
And then shaking itself loose as a Realm of the
    Buddha gone feral
Gone wild,
A Realm of Heaven
A Realm of Hell,
A Realm of Hungry Ghosts,

And so the Poet,
The Bard, and the Mage,
All who study the power of the language
Just as the musician studies the power of the tone
    and the color of the Mode
Know there is a power of transformation
Which is found in even the slightest inflection
The least nuance of meaning,
It is the vibration of the Earth
Shaped into a repeatable sound,
For "First was The Word,"
But after six days of creation
Even God needed rest
To turn off the light and climb the stairs
And forget to see – once again.

## *Kali in Morning Light*

Tantra is "To Weave,"
The weaving of what is ordinary
Into something which is extra-ordinary,
The same into the Sacred
The dull into Wisdom
The failed into The Beautiful,
It's our tears into Stairways
The spinning of straw into gold,
For love is born into our eyes as well as our heart
We cannot turn away from Life to live in a
    Sacred Way,
It is only when kindness becomes the air in which
    we breathe
That the stench of the Underworld
Turns into spring.

## *In Poppy Dreams*

It is love, wild and free,
Which enjoins you to be
Just as you are,
And I will love you in your ability
To be other than who I am
For it is, after all, a biodiversity of our delight in
    Being
Which unfetters our world
And allows it to sing,
And it is in the Songs
Which weave through each other
That color is bursted exuberantly forth into the
    greys of our world,
And it is opalescent sighs
Which are the true courage of our Warriors Path
For magic is the very strength of our Earth
Her smile,
In which She hides.

## *Integration*

There is a Monster which sometimes comes to visit me
Dressed in Human thoughts and Human feelings
When all is quiet
Raising little hairs on the back of my head
As I entertain the entity
Which, after all, is me
Is my own ghost
Haunting my ruminations with its macabre delights
Like the Dark Raven
Tapping on the "chamber door" of all my best intentions
And I need to call in my own best council once again
Whether in the Pavilion, or on The Couch
And listen to my own worst imaginings
And re-member the scattered pieces of my own
    burgeoning Self
For the weaving of light and shadow;

I Am the Warrior of my Soul
Leading the suffering and the heinous
As well as the bright-eyed child of Beauty unfolding:
The Figured Cauldron of my Ineffable Journey into the
    Whole.

## *In the Beginning*

In The Beginning is Death
For it is The Way that Life
All Life
Need die so that it may evolve in new, beautiful,
 and profound forms,
Or perhaps to just make room for all that is coming,
But it must die to do this,
And it must hunt its Self
Eat Its self
Die in so many exciting and unusual ways,
Recycle
Else it would bury its Self in its self
With no more room to experience or expand its self,
And it must live in every way imaginable
And make free entrance into what it should do
Would do,
Else it would never individualize
Taste its Truth,
It would never become anything at all but an exercise
In Godly Robotics – A Celestial Toy
No!
Life must swim through its own sea of choices,
Drown in its own Sea of Folly to find its Way
    to Wisdom – to Heart – to Beauty

It must madly tutor itself in order to live well,
And in the end
It must untutor itself in order to transcend,

But this is Madness;

Dying, They say, (The Munificent, Impeccable,
    Impossible "They"),
Is an illusion,
That this poem is incorrect
That there is no death
Only change
Which I call Death because I do not recognize myself
    when I emerge from my change
As I become caterpillar after caterpillar in my quest to fly,
And now we are discussing "Time"
Which must go forward for there to be any life at all
Or is it that there is only time for God
Because it takes time to imagine God
And God cannot exist without me
And I cannot exist without time.

## *Forgetting to Re-Member*

The measure of a great warrior is not found in
    physical prowess
The measure of a great warrior is found in the
    depth of Spiritual Strength,
In finding your Way through the Great Denial
In reconnecting with your truth
The weight of who you are in this floating Mystery
    of Life,
We must burst forth from the great bird of prey
The plundering lie which lives within the roots of
    our fears
And grows larger with the turning of our head
Our Heart
From the focus of our Brilliance
And forgetting to tell our story
Our own Myth of Life
As a wanderer amongst the Stars
Or a sojourner within our Mother's Womb of Earth
Of substance made of Light;
Only forgetting to remember once again.

## *Manifesto*

I can not believe that children born defective have but
   one chance of life and then the uniqueness of their
   song is passed into an Infinity of Silence
A flame blown out,
But then I cannot believe that there could be anything
   defective in the patterns which adorn this incredible
   Flower called Life!
Nor could I believe that any child could be counted
   less in a hierarchy of value conceived in the minds
   of men,
For what I do believe is that all creatures are doing the
   very best they can just to be who they are
And since no thing could ever be other than what it is
Then it all must be perfect,
So what then am I to do with all of these angers,
   and  mean things which do not exist except as
   imperfections in my thinking
Which by definition is perfect?
The answer will never be found within the Realms
   of Science
Nor in the Realms of Religion, or the Religion
   of Science,
But will swim forever within the lands of our
   Lady of Kindness
Our Mother of Muse.

## *Twelve Steps to Life*

I forgive the folly of my Becoming,
I can no longer lay awake at night thinking about
    my sins,
It is too much!
All of the lives I have adversely affected,
They are beyond my reach forever;

There is a Way to Happiness,
The Buddha knew this
Even if the Saints did not;

If forgiveness did not blow rampant
Across the Fields of Life,
The weight of suffering would render us inert,
Flowers would not bloom,
Birds would not sing,
I would not be able to write this poem,
And your smile would not fire my heart to
    miraculous deeds.

## *Transference*

I am dancing on the face of Eternity,
It lies just beneath my dreams
Like a shimmering pool barely deep
Barely solid beneath my feet
But my eyes do not see it
And my ears do not hear the ever deepening of its sound;

And there are Things which move in Eternity,
But they do not know that they are Things
And they do not know that they move
For when they enter My World?
They do not remember that they did not know
Their mind can not re-enter that Womb;

How is it then that All Things have only one Mother,
And live and die and scatter about
And then come to sing another song?

And the smiling countenance of that Being,
    Though Eternal,
Has gifted me its Heart
For me to unfold.

# 4AM

I've done it again,
Once again I have found my self in the Hallway
    of Mirrors
The place where Depth is Illusion,
Once again I have walked through the vale
Parted the diaphanous trace
And found myself in a land where Time smiles at me
    from the branch of a tree
Smiles like Alice's cat,
Where, If I could talk backwards
I would find my self at the beginning of things
Imagining that I could be a Poet,
It is All
All of this
Contained in the brightly lit present
In this Realm of Now
Far far away
Always Becoming, Yet ever drifting
But not one spot removed
From this Single Enchantment.

## *September*

We are so lucky to be buoyant within these realms
    of Mystery,
To be brought out of nothing to form ourselves into
    the boundaries of a personality
To personally imbibe our senses in a Treasure Hunt
    of Cosmic proportions,
But what Golden God is it which wishes to be found?
Or what Silver Womb wishes to be opened?
In this land where I know the meanings of words
But not the things described,
I reach for a larger voice,
A larger note upon the void.

*Three Poems*
*For the Almost Full Moon*
*On a January Night*

### I

I Am light-years from where I began,
I began as a bubble
But now I Am a Star,
If you saw me from afar
You would see me in my brilliance
Adorned in my Suit of Lights
The honored guest at my own nuptial feast

### II

I Am hunting along the eves of my world
Poking through the webs of the spiders who live there
And weave their spells of entrapment
Capturing those things which would try to escape my reality
And turn to haunt me from "outside,"
Things which I wouldn't want to be seen
like my childhood

Or the harm I have given to others,
The spiders catch them
They bite them and make them still,
So I Am safe to breathe-in the rarefied air of my accomplishments
Of my Holiness,
But wait!
If Brahma is Eternal
And my truth is struggling - gasping
For the fresh air of "That" Reality
Then I must strip my self of my denials
Go naked into your presence
And let you in,
But how could I live unmolested, Unharmed
Without my spiders?

## III

"Tara" is a Sanskrit word for Star,
The Mother goddess of the Himalaya
It is the Soul of a Star come to Earth

"Tara is also the Celtic word for "The Hill,'
A Bump on the earth which is the Heart of Ireland
The Seat of the High King,
The Soul of the Earth;

King and Queen,
The power of Heart
And the Celestial power of Light
All contained within a flick of the tongue

## The Flavor of Me

I Am mixed in this natural world,
Mixed and stirred within it
I Am spiced and cooked
Seasoned to perfection,
And though the illumination is yet to come
It is the flavor of Me
Which will add to this feast of life
This banquet of Earth
Which the Gods (Goddesses) attend with regularity
Tasting the fruits of their labors
Endlessly cavorting in this garden of delights.

*Mother Tara*
*Who Has a Heart as Big as*
*The Sky*

Could we have guessed?
That all the highways and byways
Cities and States,
Homes and Horses and Fresh TV's,
And all of the masses reaching for
A Way to Love,
And a destination home
With deer that walk through the front yard
And coyotes who sing in a night so quiet
That your thinking and your breathing
Have equal volume,
And planets,
And stars within whole universes of Being
Who express their astronomical distances
And the gargantuan weight of their Soul
In a small smile of contentment
That plays upon our lips
As we touch hands,and lean into each other
And sigh;
Because it is so good just to be us.

## *I Will*

I will sit forever at this desert crossroads
Watching the road ahead come together in a small dot
First in one direction and then in the other,
I will sit behind the wheel of this smooth driving car
Staring off in the distance
While heat waves ripple upon the asphalt
Forming pools like water
As if some "Thing" could rise-up and say, "Hello,"
I will sit here and watch for this
While wiser men
With pens in their pockets,
Rising up above the line of their heart,
In Reds and Blacks and Blues
Will crinkle their brows, and rub their chins
And ruminate about the condition my condition is in.

## *The Guiding Force*

The tempest did not come in from the sea
It rose-up from a deeper place within the Earth,
It rose-up from out of that ocean which I inhabit
And call "Me,"
And I swear that I did not see it coming,
And the shores of my smugness which I felt to be
    so solid,
The deep foundations of my Estate
Where-in I dwelt as the irrefutable Myth of Me,
Was broken and crushed like a candy box of card
    The gummys of my life
Tossed and scattered by the winds
And never again,
Should I find my way home
And re-member about the core of my beliefs,
Will I ever turn my face in arrogance
To the raw forces of my nature
And feel that I am immune and safe from their storm,
The weather of who I Am.

## *The Nature of What is Lost*

In the still of the night
When the lamp has burned low
And the fire is one half asleep in dully burning embers,
In this quiet time
When I am sitting in my big stuffed chair
And the dog is whining and twitching in his sleep,
Ah…
This is the time when I can see them
I catch them in the corner of my eye
Passing through
Huge winged shadows which are leaving my world
Passing through into their own darkness
Into their own obscurity
Taking with them vast and fantastic treasures which
    belong to them alone,
Wisdom's and Arts. Beauty, and Grace of Being
And the special evolved loneliness of a culture which is
Their own completely special way of touching Life,
Forever lost in their flight into death
In the quieting of their words and their song;
For these are large creatures which are dying
Whole systems of Life,

Peoples and cultures and Races of Being
with languages that name things which no other
    language sees,
And when the eyes of these words are closed
And the silence of their tongues is thorough
Then worlds will turn up missing
And the Magic of their Dreams will slip away
    unnoticed
And maybe also, the answer to our cries
But then, we shall never know.

## *Natural Selection*

I have been naturally selected to be with you
To hold you close through long winter nights
To hold you close into the quickening light of
    Spring
Into the full warmth of Summer
When all of our dreams fall ripely into our hands,
Naturally selected to have the children that we do,
To watch them grow,
To watch them struggle and triumph
In trying to make sense out of Being Alive;
To naturally select their own mates
To have their own children
To see over the borders of their lives
Into a Great World
Turning in its own rising sentience
Holding close to its Heart
Its own Wings of Life
Where millions of years pass all to quickly
And are gone;
For even the Heavens age
Become grandparents to planets and stars
Naturally selecting – Some day
A new Universe,
Or perhaps a new grain of sand to pass between
    my toes.

## *Pennyweight in Browser*

Everything must weigh the same,
Time and pain must weigh the same
As love and space
Or trees, rocks, feathers, and ideas,
Peoples and penguins,
We must all weigh the same
Because we are all falling through Eternity at
    the same rate of speed
And The Piper continues to play his tune
And all things are where we left them
But a moment ago.

## Left Turn to Center

How is it?
That in a world where everything eats everything
I can believe in Beauty,
And how is it?
When cruelty is consciously spread across the
    Fields of Life
I can place Kindness upon my Altar,
It is not a defiance of Reality
(And what is Real at any rate?)
But a Belief that,
At long last
All things shall be rectified into a Present
A Now in which all suffering has never occurred
Never Occurred!
And so the Beauty and the Kindness
Which I seek
Has never been in other than Here,
In this Moment Forever,
So...
I Am the suffering
Or,
I Am the Redemption
For How could I live with my Self, Being God,
If I could not Rectify The Folly
Of my own burgeoning humanness
Becoming Truly, Really Me.

## *Seeking a Planetary Presence*

I am looking forward into the days of my youth
It is perhaps something that older people do,
The stars still shine there as they do here
Above my head,
The Sun hangs buttery in the endless still heat
    of Summer
And Winter has traveled far
Far from my hands which show the lines and
    creases of long continued use
And my fingertips which reach deep into my psyche
But find no bottom to touch
And no Soul to squeeze between them
But Infinite expanding life
Making this life on Earth
A pimple
Bursting forth kudos to The Dreamer of it all,
Well Done!
Well Done!

## *In the Realm of Hungry Ghosts*

We have not yet seen the final result of this mad rushing
    about
This no time for nothing,
Nor have we yet seen the extent of the fearsome results of
This deprivation of nothing upon the Soul of the world
For it is nothing which is lacking
In this plague o Hungry Ghosts
Who can never stop consuming for they are never
    nourished by what they eat,
But should this grasping ever be finished,
Should this grasping ever be done,
Then all would be quiet
And silence, for a time,
Would bud upon the Earth
And the small and furry things
Would peep out their faces from where they have hidden
The songs of birds would fill the opalescence
    of our thoughts
And the crunch of gravel
The snap of twigs,
Would be heard, once again, as we travel on.

*Preface to Monsoon:*

The Monsoon <u>is</u> the desert
The desert defines it
It powers it
It is too intense to be called, "beautiful"
It moves into another realm than that.

I wanted the desert to be seen
Wrapped around and twined into the monsoon
through the teeth of its weather
Though the parched eye of its coyotes

For it is Real – This Tale
I wanted it to be told
For it will happen again
It will always happen
It occupies that space.

## *Monsoon*

And the heat bears down so that
One would not think that light could weigh so
 heavily upon the flesh,
But then, One would not think at all
Enclosed in this gritty sounding breath of the swamp
    cooler
Which from its own bowels throws a sticky wet soup
    into the air
For one to breath,
For one to gulp,
To suck-in
Not cool, but cooler than not,
Cooler than what waits beyond the door,
And cooler than this T-shirt which sticks against my skin,
But then the clouds begin to gather,
Dark and Swollen,
Is it damper?
Fresher?
There is a sudden burst of hope as you turn off the
    cooler and step outside,
But hope is gone
Crushed in the pressure which begins to steadily build,

It is like a pot placed upon the stove
But it is not the stove
It is behind your eyes in the hollows of your head,
And the light of the day turns to a dull yellow,
The color of a small watt bulb in the confines of a
    desert toilet
Settled behind the laundromat at the crossroads of
    SR. 12 and Hwy. 91,
Miles and miles from nowhere,
Alive with bugs
Who have traveled a great distance to ram themselves
    against its dull light,
Mixed with the smell of such places,
And the spiders!
Huge!
Who taunt you with beady eyes to place your
    bottom upon the crusty seat as you perform
    your need and await your fate,
But now the lightning has begun to flash,
Sometimes down,
But sometimes horizontally across the sky,
An electric tear which oozes ozone,

That stings the nose,
And sharpens the sweat which creeps into the eyes,
While the pressure continues to build,
And the wind rushes up from the earth
Ripping off roofs,
Filling the air with dust and debris
And the mouth with sand,
And in the distance you hear the wail of a
    disheartened Soul
Driven Mad. Pleading for relief.
But the pressure only continues to build
Until finally!
Thunder so intense that it almost throws you to the
    ground
And a rain so loud on the tin roof of the Motel that it
    drowns out your own scream of relief
Your eyes incredulous at the sudden proliferation of
    torrents, rivers, and waterfalls, everywhere you look!
The wealth of water pouring off of roofs,
Shed roofs, car roofs, house roofs, the roofs of the
    abodes of dogs,
And up in the mountains
A lone black sedan races at insane speed down the road

As only feet behind it a raging froth of water crosses
the road yet again on its wild plunge to the antediluvian
fan of gravel and sand which awaits it thousands of
feet below,

And at the next corner
It is caught,
Tossed into the maelstrom
Flipped end over end like a child's toy
To be found later at the bottom of the hills
Arms and legs akimbo,
Steaming, not moving, in the afternoon sun,
For he had only gone into the mountains to think,
Feeling safe in his expensive car,
Driving into the mountains in defiance of the Gods of
    the darkening light,
Who, Had they been able,
Would have laughed at his folly,
For even though – long ago
They had lost their Names,
In this Dance,
This feral orgy of energies,
This ejaculation of sheets of wet rain

Of wind and ozone smells
And sounds of primal climax,
They had lost none of the Power
Which makes us small.

OTHER BOOKS
BY
CRAIG WILLIAM ANDREWS

*A Song In Amber*

*Some Things Gentle*
*Some Things Kind*

www.ingramcontent.com/pod-product-compliance
Lightning Source LLC
Chambersburg PA
CBHW022124040426
42450CB00006B/839